D1372276

KNOW YOUR FOOD

FLAVORINGS, COLORINGS, AND PRESERVATIVES

KNOW YOUR FOOD

Fats and Cholesterol

Fiber

Flavorings, Colorings, and Preservatives

Food Safety

Genetically Modified Foods

Gluten

Organic Foods

Protein

Salt

Starch and Other Carbohydrates

Sugar and Sweeteners

Vitamins and Minerals

Water

KNOW YOUR FOOD

Flavorings, Colorings, and Preservatives

JOHN PERRITANO

MASON CREST

Mason Crest
450 Parkway Drive, Suite D
Broomall, PA 19008
www.masoncrest.com

MTM Publishing, Inc.
435 West 23rd Street, #8C
New York, NY 10011
www.mtmpublishing.com

President: Valerie Tomaselli
Vice President, Book Development: Hilary Poole
Designer: Annemarie Redmond
Copyeditor: Peter Jaskowiak
Editorial Assistant: Leigh Eron

Series ISBN: 978-1-4222-3733-5
Hardback ISBN: 978-1-4222-3736-6
E-Book ISBN: 978-1-4222-8043-0

Library of Congress Cataloging-in-Publication Data
Names: Perritano, John, author.
Title: Flavorings, colorings, and preservatives / by John Perritano.
Description: Broomall, PA: Mason Crest, [2018] | Series: Know your food |
    Audience: Ages 12+. | Audience: Grades 7 to 8. | Includes bibliographical
    references index.
Identifiers: LCCN 2016053140 (print) | LCCN 2016055591 (ebook) | ISBN
    9781422237366 (hardback: alk. paper) | ISBN 9781422280430 (ebook)
Subjects: LCSH: Food additives—Juvenile literature. | Coloring matter in
    food—Juvenile literature. | Food industry and trade—Juvenile literature.
Classification: LCC TX553.A3 P386 2018 (print) | LCC TX553.A3 (ebook) | DDC
    641.3/08—dc23
LC record available at https://lccn.loc.gov/2016053140

Printed and bound in the United States of America.

First printing
9 8 7 6 5 4 3 2 1

TABLE OF CONTENTS

Key Icons to Look for:

Words to Understand: These words with their easy-to-understand definitions will increase the reader's understanding of the text, while building vocabulary skills.

Sidebars: This boxed material within the main text allows readers to build knowledge, gain insights, explore possibilities, and broaden their perspectives by weaving together additional information to provide realistic and holistic perspectives.

Educational Videos: Readers can view videos by scanning our QR codes, which will provide them with additional educational content to supplement the text. Examples include news coverage, moments in history, speeches, iconic sports moments, and much more.

Text-Dependent Questions: These questions send the reader back to the text for more careful attention to the evidence presented there.

Research Projects: Readers are pointed toward areas of further inquiry connected to each chapter. Suggestions are provided for projects that encourage deeper research and analysis.

Series Glossary of Key Terms: This back-of-the-book glossary contains terminology used throughout the series. Words found here increase the reader's ability to read and comprehend higher-level books and articles in this field.

SERIES INTRODUCTION

In the early 19th century, a book was published in France called *Physiologie du goût* (*The Physiology of Taste*), and since that time, it has never gone out of print. Its author was Jean Anthelme Brillat-Savarin. Brillat-Savarin is still considered to be one of the great food writers, and he was, to use our current lingo, arguably the first "foodie." Among other pearls, *Physiologie du goût* gave us one of the quintessential aphorisms about dining: "Tell me what you eat, and I will tell you what you are."

This concept was introduced to Americans in the 20th century by a nutritionist named Victor Lindlahr, who wrote simply, "You are what you eat." Lindlahr interpreted the saying literally: if you eat healthy food, he argued, you will become a healthy person.

But Brillat-Savarin likely had something a bit more metaphorical in mind. His work suggested that the dishes we create and consume have not only nutritional implications, but ethical, philosophical, and even political implications, too.

To be clear, Brillat-Savarin had a great deal to say on the importance of nutrition. In his writings he advised people to limit their intake of "floury and starchy substances," and for that reason he is sometimes considered to be the inventor of the low-carb diet. But Brillat-Savarin also took the idea of dining extremely seriously. He was devoted to the notion of pleasure in eating and was a fierce advocate of the importance of being a good host. In fact, he went so far as to say that anyone who doesn't make an effort to feed his guests "does not deserve to have friends." Brillat-Savarin also understood that food was at once deeply personal and extremely social. "Cooking is one of the oldest arts," he wrote, "and one that has rendered us the most important service in civic life."

Modern diners and cooks still grapple with the many implications of Brillat-Savarin's most famous statement. Certainly on a nutritional level, we understand that a diet that's low in fat and high in whole grains is a key to healthy living. This is no minor issue. Unless our current course is reversed, today's "obesity epidemic" is poised to significantly reduce the life spans of future generations.

Meanwhile, we are becoming increasingly aware of how the decisions we make at supermarkets can ripple outward, impacting our neighborhoods, nations, and the earth as a whole. Increasing numbers of us are demanding organically produced foods and ethically sourced ingredients. Some shoppers reject products that contain artificial ingredients like trans fats or high-fructose corn syrup. Some adopt gluten-free or vegan diets, while others "go Paleo" in the hopes of returning to a more "natural" way of eating. A simple trip to the supermarket can begin to feel like a personality test—the implicit question is not only "what does a *healthy* person eat?," but also "what does a *good* person eat?"

The Know Your Food series introduces students to these complex issues by looking at the various components that make up our meals: carbohydrates, fats, proteins, vitamins, and so on. Each volume focuses on one component and explains its function in our bodies, how it gets into food, how it changes when cooked, and what happens when we consume too much or too little. The volumes also look at food production—for example, how did the food dye called Red No. 2 end up in our food, and why was it taken out? What are genetically modified organisms, and are they safe or not? Along the way, the volumes also explore different diets, such as low-carb, low-fat, vegetarian, and gluten-free, going beyond the hype to examine their potential benefits and possible downsides.

Each chapter features definitions of key terms for that specific section, while a Series Glossary at the back provides an overview of words that are most important to the set overall. Chapters have Text-Dependent Questions at the end, to help students assess their comprehension of the most important material, as well as suggested Research Projects that will help them continue their exploration. Last but not least, QR codes accompany each chapter; students with cell phones or tablets can scan these codes for videos that will help bring the topics to life. (Those without devices can access the videos via an Internet browser; the addresses are included at the end of the Further Reading list.)

In the spirit of Brillat-Savarin, the volumes in this set look beyond nutrition to also consider various historical, political, and ethical aspects of food. Whether it's the key role that sugar played in the slave trade, the implications of industrial meat production in the fight against climate change, or the short-sighted political decisions that resulted in the water catastrophe in Flint, Michigan, the Know Your Food series introduces students to the ways in which a meal can be, in a real sense, much more than just a meal.

TYPES OF ADDITIVES

WORDS TO UNDERSTAND

emulsifiers: chemicals that allow mixtures to blend.

extract: concentrated component of food.

impervious: resistant to allowing fluid to pass through.

rancid: awful smelling.

synthetic: human-made.

In 1976, a chemistry teacher named Roger Bennatti conducted a science experiment. He gave his students at George Stevens Academy in the coastal Maine town of Blue Hills a handful of money and sent them to the store to buy a package of Twinkies. When the pupils returned, Bennatti ate one of the golden cream-filled cakes and put the other (Twinkies come in packages of two) on the top of the blackboard.

Bennatti then instructed his students to observe what changes occurred to the treat over time. Twinkies had a reputation as a seemingly indestructible food overloaded with additives and preservatives. Although made mostly of flour and sugar, the Twinkie contained about 36 ingredients, including polysorbate 60, one in a class of substances used in cosmetics.

Bennatti's goal was to see how long a preserved food could last before it turned into a moldy green goo or disintegrated into inedible dust. The years came and went. Students studied, did their homework, and graduated. Bennatti retired in 2004. All the while the Twinkie remained in the classroom under a glass case, seemingly impervious to air, moisture, bacteria, and everything else that causes food to decay.

The Blue Hills snack was a celebrity of sorts, known as "the world's oldest Twinkie." Hostess, the maker of Twinkies and other snacks, went bankrupt in 2012 and announced it was going to stop baking the cakes (another company would resume production).

Four years later, the Blue Hills Twinkie that had supposedly had a shelf life of only 25 days turned 40 years old. It was still well preserved, although time had

Manufacturers add preservatives to foods so that they can sit on shelves for longer periods of time without spoiling.

WHAT'S REALLY IN A TWINKIE

The author Steve Ettlinger spent an enormous amount of time researching what was really inside the Twinkie. In his book *Twinkie, Deconstructed*, Ettlinger says the main ingredients, besides flour, are several types of added sugar—specifically high fructose corn syrup, dextrose, and glucose. In addition to making the cake taste sweet, sugar provides color and retains moisture that improves the snack's shelf life.

According to Ettlinger, there are no eggs in Twinkies to stabilize the cake batter or to make it last longer on the store shelf. Instead, bakers infuse the cake with monoglycerides and diglycerides (both fatty acids). They also use polysorbate 60 (made from sugar alcohol and ethylene oxide, which comes from crude oil). The compound does a variety of jobs, including helping the cake retain water. That's partly why Twinkies are so moist and their filling is so creamy. There is no butter in a Twinkie. Instead, the cake gets its buttery flavor from diacetyl, an organic, yellow-green compound used in microwave popcorn. Believe it or not, there's only one true preservative in the snack—sorbic acid, a natural organic compound.

faded its bright yellow color and caused its outer shell to flake. The cake was less than spongy. Still, the Twinkie was mostly intact—although, to be fair, probably indigestible (no one ate it to find out).

The story of the world's oldest Twinkie is the story of additives and synthetic ingredients that food makers add to the things we eat and drink. Natural ingredients such as milk, butter, and eggs spoil rather quickly. Yet when combined with an assortment of chemicals, food gets a new lease on life. It stays fresh longer and seldom loses its color or shape. Some additives even make food taste better.

But there can be a downside: you are what you eat, or so goes the old saying. The problem is many people don't know what they are eating these days.

WHY ADDITIVES?

For centuries, people have tried to find new ways to preserve food and improve its flavor. Some of their methods have included adding salt, sugar, vinegar, spices, and herbs. But as the world's population grew, people no longer had to time to grow or preserve what they ate. Still, they wanted food that was safe, tasty, and nutritious. As food processing became more industrialized, scientists found a number of ways to improve food's texture, flavor, color, and nutritional value. They invented additives, including artificial preservatives, colors, and flavorings.

The U.S. Food and Drug Administration (FDA), the government agency responsible for making sure food is safe in the United States, has a database of thousands of food additives. The FDA's official definition states that additives are "any substance the intended use of which results or may reasonably be expected to result—directly or indirectly—in its becoming a component or otherwise affecting the characteristics of any food."

To put it more simply, food additives are any ingredient added to preserve freshness, maintain safety, improve nutritional value, or to enhance food's taste, texture, or appearance. Preservatives, for example, slow the process by which food spoils, resulting in a longer shelf life. Preservatives also fight against foodborne illnesses, such as E. coli and botulism. Some preservatives prevent oils and fats from turning rancid.

Artificial sweeteners and flavors make food taste better. Artificial colors improve the look of food, making it more appetizing. Stabilizers, emulsifiers, and thickeners improve food texture, while other ingredients help cakes, pies, and other baked goods rise in the oven. Some additives minimize acidity, while others reduce fat. Still others make food more nutritious.

Emulsifiers help give ice cream its smooth texture.

There are two types of additives: direct and indirect. Direct additives are added directly during the baking or cooking process. For example, makers of salad dressings add xanthan gum to thicken their products. Beverage companies add high fructose corn syrup, a sweetener synthesized from corn, to give their drinks a sweet taste.

EDUCATIONAL VIDEO

ADDITIVE BASICS

Scan this code for a video about food additives.

Indirect additives make their way into food during processing, packaging, and handling. Indirect additives are usually found in small amounts. For example, polyethylene terephthalate, or PET, is a plastic that protects food from oxygen and carbon dioxide, helping it to say fresh. Beverage companies use PET when bottling water, soda, juices, and other drinks. Microwave food trays are also made from PET. When food is packaged in PET containers, tiny traces of the substance make their way into the product.

Figuring out whether such additives are safe to consume is a tough job. Scientific studies can often be incomplete. As a result, scientists at the FDA and elsewhere have to make an educated guess about which additives are safe. The agency regulates how food makers use additives and in what amount. It also determines how the chemicals should be identified on food labels.

COLORINGS, PRESERVATIVES, AND FLAVORINGS

The three main types of additives are colorings, preservatives, and flavorings. According to the FDA, color additives can include any "dye, pigment or substance, which when applied to a food . . . is capable of imparting color." Artificial colors are the reason why Froot Loops, Lucky Charms, and snack foods like Reese's Pieces, M&Ms, and, yes, Twinkies are so colorful.

Food colorings can come from natural sources, including plant **extracts**. Others are made in the laboratory, usually from petroleum-based chemicals. These chemicals

Artificial colorings can be used to give foods a hue that is not found in nature.

(the FDA has only approved nine of them) give food a uniform color, and when mixed together, they can provide a variety of hues.

Chemical colorings are less expensive to use than natural colors. Sometimes food manufacturers can only use certain dyes for specific foods. Hot dogs, for example, are shades of orange because sausage makers can only use Orange B to give casings their tint. Over the years, the government has banned various food dyes because of toxicity or possible carcinogenic, or cancer-causing, effects.

Preservatives slow the process by which food spoils. Food turns rotten for many reasons, especially when it comes in contact with oxygen and moisture. Both provide fertile breeding grounds for some microorganisms, including bacteria, molds, and yeasts. Moisture fosters chemical reactions between food ingredients that can result in rancid tastes and unappetizing textures. Certain enzymes can also speed up the spoilage process, as can temperature and light.

Preservatives, such those made from sulfur, can slow or stop the growth of bacteria, molds, and yeasts. As a result, preservatives stop bacteria from contaminating food. Some of that bacteria can make a person sick. Nitrate-based compounds, which are routinely added to sausages and hams, also protect against foodborne illnesses, including botulism, as do calcium, benzoic acid, potassium salts, and other chemicals.

In addition to artificial colorings and preservatives, processed food is laden with artificial chemicals that mimic natural flavors. Flavor is not the same thing as taste. Flavor is a perception by which we use our senses—mainly smell—to determine a particular food flavor. In fact, about 80 percent of what we "taste" is determined by how food smells. Taste, on the other hand, is determined by our ability to detect sourness, sweetness, bitterness, and saltiness.

Chemicals—natural and synthetic—determine food's flavor. When you pick an apple off a tree and bite into it, dozens of chemicals inside the apple interact to create the apple's taste and smell. The distinctive smell of clover comes from the chemical eugenol. Cinnamon gets its unique flavor from cinnamaldehyde, a carbon-, oxygen-, and hydrogen-based compound.

Real vanilla flavoring is made from the vanilla plant, but doing so is time consuming and expensive. One way manufacturers address this is to use some real vanilla and combine it with an additive such as corn syrup.

Producing artificial flavorings is less expensive than using natural flavorings, which is why food manufacturers use them. Vanilla, for example, is an extremely expensive natural flavor. Workers need to extract natural vanillin from an orchid native to Mexico, a process that takes time and money. Making synthetic vanilla, however, is less time consuming and does not cost as much. There is often a taste difference between real and artificial flavorings. For instance, real vanilla has a much more robust taste than artificial vanilla.

17

NO FRUIT IN FROOT LOOPS!

Froot Loops and Trix are two cereals that are fun to look at, and even more fun to eat. The multicolored cereals have been a staple of breakfast tables for decades. Yet there is actually no fruit in either of them. Each has a variety of colorful dyes that give the cereals their color, but they all taste pretty much the same. FoodBeast.com did a blind taste test of Froot Loops and determined that all the loops tasted the same, regardless of their color. The same held true for Trix and Fruity Pebbles.

No fruit was harmed in the making of this cereal.

NUTRITIONAL ADDITIVES

In many cases, food makers will add vitamins and minerals to their products. There are a few reasons why this happens. One is that nutritional additives restore any nutritional value that might have been destroyed during the production process.

TYPES OF ADDITIVES

Adding nutrients to food began in 1924, when scientists added iodine to table salt to prevent neck swelling due to the enlargement of the body's thyroid gland. Since that time, companies have been adding vitamins and minerals to foods—especially vitamins A and D to dairy and cereal products, and vitamin C to certain beverages. Folic acid has been a nutritional success story. Added to cold cereals, flour, breads, pasta, baked goods and crackers, folic acid prevents a variety of ailments, including anemia. It also helps prevent heart disease, stroke, and other conditions.

Pregnant women take folic acid to prevent birth defects such as spina bifida, a condition that occurs when the spine of a fetus doesn't form properly. A reduction in these types of birth defects has been attributed partly to the addition of folic acid to many foods. Ironically, scientists are now studying the role that *excess* folic acid may play in the developmental condition called autism.

TEXT-DEPENDENT QUESTIONS

1. What are synthetic food ingredients?
2. What are the three main types of food additives?
3. What are the differences between a direct and indirect additive?

RESEARCH PROJECT

Go into your cupboard, pantry, refrigerator, or freezer and select one of your favorite prepackaged foods. Find the label on the container and write down the ingredients. Indicate which ingredients are natural or synthetic. Use the Internet to research each ingredient. Next, write down how your opinion of that food might have changed after your investigation.

CHAPTER 2

HISTORY, MANUFACTURE, AND USE

 ## WORDS TO UNDERSTAND

antimicrobial: substances that kill disease-carrying bacteria.

brine: water that contains a significant amount of salt.

hormone: a substance produced by the body that helps cells do their job.

muckraking: investigative reporting during the late 19th and early 20th centuries.

oxidation: changes that occur when a substance is exposed to oxygen.

pathogens: a bacterium, virus, or other microorganism that can cause disease.

Preserving food is not a modern idea; in fact, the practice goes back centuries. By its very nature, food begins to spoil the moment a person plucks a grape from a vine, cracks open an egg, or filets a fish. Our ancient ancestors had to find ways—usually through trial and error—of preserving the foods they caught, harvested, and grew. In fact, figuring out how preserve foods was a key step in human progress, enabling hunters and gatherers to settle down, grow crops, build cities, and form great civilizations.

21

The methods of food preservation varied and were often dictated by where a person lived. For example, people who lived in frigid regions found freezing seal, caribou, bear, reindeer, and fish meat to be a good preservation method. On the other hand, people in warmer climates dried fruits, meats, and vegetables in the sun and wind.

SALT AS A PRESERVATIVE

The ancient Egyptians, always on the cutting edge of technology, figured out that using salt—which was bountiful in northern Africa—was a great way to preserve fish. Salt absorbs water from foods, creating a hostile environment for mold and bacteria. Although the Egyptians might not have known the science behind salting, the practice was so important to Egyptian society that priests were the only ones allowed to do it. The Egyptians also used salt in the mummification process as a way to keep corpses from decaying.

Enhancing the flavor of food was also a prime objective of the Egyptians. They used honey, dates, and raisins as sweeteners.

FERMENTATION, PICKLING, SMOKING

Fermentation is another ancient preservation method. Fermentation is the process by which microorganisms in starches and sugars turn into alcohol. Although fermentation was probably discovered by accident, early humans used the process to turn fruits into wine, grains into beer, and foods such as cabbage into sauerkraut or kimchi.

Beer, a product of grain fermentation, was nutritious and essential to a good diet. Fermentation forced the microorganisms in the brew's grain to manufacture vitamins and alcohol. Fermentation also killed disease-causing pathogens, making the beverage safer to drink than most potable (drinkable) water. In fact, when beer began to run out on the *Mayflower* in 1620, the passengers began getting sick. As soon as they could, the Pilgrims landed at Plymouth Rock so they could brew more beer.

Kimchi is a spicy pickled cabbage that is associated with Korean cuisine, but it is becoming increasingly popular around the world.

Pickling is another ancient preservation method. The Romans were experts in pickling foods in acids such as vinegar. When sugar ferments, it turns first into an alcohol, and then, through the oxidation of certain bacteria, into acetic acid. The acid kills bacteria. When wine, cider, or beer soured, people poured the brine into jugs or pots and then added different foods. The Romans also used natural preservatives like potassium nitrate to not only preserve food, but also enhance taste and appearance.

Smoking food over a fire prevented the growth of microbes by reducing moisture, allowing the meat to remain edible for a long period. The chemicals in the smoke—including alcohol and formaldehyde—also preserved the meat.

A production line at a contemporary meat cannery.

THE POISON SQUAD

As the world's population increased, so did the need to find different ways to preserve food. Salting, smoking, pickling, fermenting, freeze-drying, canning, and even pasteurization (the process of heating food at high temperatures to kill bacteria) could do only so much.

As the food business became more industrialized, food makers looked for new preservation methods. By the beginning of the 20th century, processed foods, especially meats, canned vegetables, and other products, had become increasingly popular. They were easy to manufacture, transport, and use. Some of the chemical additives, however, were not safe. But since there was very little government oversight, food makers did what they wanted, even though their actions made a lot of people sick. Activists and **muckraking** journalists railed against the food industry for using unsafe additives.

Upton Sinclair's novel *The Jungle*, for example, exposed the unhealthy standards used by the meatpacking industry. This passage sums up the true nature of the food industry's disregard for health standards:

> *The meat would be shoveled into carts, and the man who did the shoveling would not trouble to lift out a rat even when he saw one—there were things that went into the sausage in comparison with which a poisoned rat was a tidbit. There was no place for the men to wash their hands before they ate their dinner, and so they made a practice of washing them in the water that was to be ladled into the sausage.*

EDUCATIONAL VIDEO

CANNING

Scan this code for a video about the history of canning food.

The Poison Squad, led by Harvey Wiley, tested the safety of food on themselves. They invented their own, pun-laden slogan.

At the time, the states—not the federal government—were charged with food oversight, and most of those laws dated back to colonial times. Finally, in 1902, Dr. Harvey W. Wiley, the chief chemist at the U.S. Department of Agriculture's Bureau of Chemistry, set off on an investigation to figure out which additives were safe and which were not.

With the approval of Congress, Wiley recruited a group of volunteers, soon to be called the "Poison Squad," and began to study the effects of certain chemicals and substances. The "twelve young clerks," all men, of the Poison Squad, promised to eat food prepared only in the Poison's Squad's kitchen. If they got sick or died—well, each person knew the risks.

Before every meal, the Poison Squad carefully weighed themselves and checked their body temperature and pulse rates. Wiley collected their stool, sweat, hair and urine samples. Each person ate foods containing a variety of chemical additives, including borax, formaldehyde, and salicylic acid, a drug that is today used to treat a variety of skin disorders, such as acne, dandruff, and psoriasis.

At the time, Borax was the most common food preservative. Meatpackers used the mineral to make rotting meat seem as if it was edible. For eight months, the Poison Squad ate foods laced with borax, including applesauce, turkey, canned string beans, and sweet potatoes. Many got sick with headaches, stomachaches, and other maladies.

One by one, Wiley and the Poison Squad demonstrated the ill-health effects of several additives. When the experiments were over, Wiley advocated that food manufacturers use chemicals only when necessary and only if they were deemed safe to consume.

Partly because of Wiley's work, Congress passed the Pure Food and Drug Act of 1906, which mandated "the examinations of specimens of foods and drugs shall

A FEW FOOD PRESERVATIVES

This list highlights some common food preservatives.

- *Methylcyclopropene*: This is a gas that stops apples and other fruits from rotting. It stops fruit from producing a natural **hormone** called ethylene, which causes food to ripen. The chemical can keep apples fresh for up to a year, and bananas for up to a month.

- *Nitrates*. These are inorganic salts found in large deposits. Often found in human-made fertilizers, nitrates not only kill bacteria, but they also give processed meat and fish a red color.

- *Sodium benzoate*. Most commonly found in milk, meat products, and cereals, sodium benzoate kills fungi.

- *Sulfites*. These naturally occurring preservatives are often found in wine, dried fruit, and dried potato products. In winemaking, sulfites can stop the oxidation process, which stops the growth of bacteria.

be made in the Bureau of Chemistry of the Department of Agriculture, or under the direction and supervision of such Bureau, for the purpose of determining from such examinations whether such articles are adulterated or misbranded." It was the first of many food and drug laws the U.S. government has passed to ensure that food and food additives are safe.

PRESERVATIVES AND THEIR USES

Preservatives not only keep food fresher longer, but they are also vital to the safety of the food supply. The Centers for Disease Control and Prevention (CDC) estimates that 48 million people in the United States become sick or are hospitalized every year because of foodborne illnesses. Some 3,000 ultimately die. A number of pathogens are responsible for most deaths, especially *norovirus*, a contagion that can inflame the stomach and intestines. Each year, the CDC says, 5.46 million people contract the virus, many by touching contaminated surfaces. Another bacteria, *salmonella*, accounts for about 1 million illnesses.

To help prevent these and other illnesses, food makers put various antimicrobial chemicals into their products. Antimicrobial additives prevent bacteria from settling and growing on food. Some, such as oregano, cinnamon, and basil oil, are natural, while others are made in a laboratory. Organic acids, such as lactic, acetic, and citric acid, are popular natural antimicrobials that are often combined with other compounds. For example, potassium sorbate, along with lactic and citric acid, kills the bacteria that cause salmonella. Benzoic acid and sodium benzoate (a type of salt) slow yeast and mold from growing in fruit juices and on other fruit products.

The poultry industry uses chlorine dioxide, an indirect additive, to treat water used in the processing of poultry, while meat packagers use sodium nitrate to stabilize the "red" color of meat and fish, but also to control various forms of bacteria.

The herb oregano has natural antimicrobial properties.

ARTIFICIAL FLAVORS AND THEIR USES

As noted in chapter one, chemical flavorings can be made from either natural sources or in a laboratory. Artificial flavorings are often cheaper to produce than extracting flavorings form natural sources. However, the distinction between "natural" and "artificial" is not nearly as black and white as it might seem. Even "natural" flavorings are frequently made in laboratories. Scientists combine natural chemicals found in food to make "natural" flavors, and they mix "synthetic" chemicals to make "artificial" flavors.

Moreover, some artificial flavors, such as *amyl acetate,* are synthesized from natural flavors—in this case, bananas. In fact, that's true for many artificial flavors. Before a scientist develops a laboratory-made flavor, say for a new type of coconut candy, he or she researches what chemicals are in real coconuts. Researchers then recreate that chemical in the laboratory.

Monosodium glutamate, or MSG, is a type of salt that's used as a flavor enhancer. It first synthesized in the early 1900s after a Japanese scientist isolated a chemical (glutamate) from kombu, a certain species of seaweed. Cooks routinely used the seaweed to improve the flavor of certain dishes.

Some artificial flavors were discovered by accident. Aspartame, for example, is an artificial sweetener developed by a researcher in 1965 who was working on a treatment for stomach ulcers.

Dried kombu. The flavor enhancer called MSG was synthesized based on kombu's flavor.

BIOTECH FLAVORINGS

Scientists have begun to create flavorings, such as vanilla and saffron, by genetically altering bacteria, fungi, and yeasts. These so-called biotech flavorings are genetically modified to taste and smell just like the real thing. Supporters of bio-flavors say the products might be more natural than those derived from natural chemicals.

ARTIFICIAL COLORINGS

Nothing puts a smile on a kid's face faster than diving into a big bowl of multicolored candy and washing it down with a cool glass of red fruit juice. Part of the reason these foods are fun to eat is because they're are colorful—thanks to artificial dyes.

Color can make food more appealing. In fact, many of the most popular foods on the grocery store shelf, including fruits, brownies, cheeses, and taco chips, contain artificial colors. Adding color to food is not a new thing. Centuries ago, people used natural colorings that came from minerals, fruits, and vegetables. At the height of the Industrial Revolution, for example, confectioners colored sweets with red lead, white lead, copper sulfate, and copper arsenite, among other additives.

By the mid- to late 1800s, scientists started mixing synthetic dyes. The first was mauve, discovered in 1856 by William Henry Perkin. Mauve and other food colorings were made from the by-products of coal processing and were commonly called "coal-tar" colors. Food manufacturers nefariously used coal-tar colors to hide the poor quality of their food. By the late 1800s, food makers started using different color additives for ketchups, jellies, mustards, and wines.

By 1906, however, things had begun to change, thanks to Dr. Wiley at the U.S. Department of Agriculture. At that time, the United States put in place the first restrictions on color additives, banning those "injurious to health."

For the next 30 years, government scientists tested and banned color after color. By the 1940s, the government had pared its list of approved artificial colors down to 15. Today, there are only nine approved for use in the United States, although there are several more pigments derived from natural sources, including vegetables and fruits.

WHAT'S YOUR FAVORITE (ARTIFICIAL) COLOR?

This list shows the approved FDA synthetic food dyes, along with some of the foods you will find them in.

Straight color	Year approved	Some food uses
Blue No. 1	1969	baked goods, beverages, candies, cereal
Blue No. 2	1987	candy, beverages, pet food
Green No. 3	1982	ice cream, sorbet, candy
Orange B	1966	sausage casings, hot dogs
Citrus Red No. 2	1963	skins of oranges not intended or used for processing
Red No. 3	1969	sausage casings, maraschino cherries, baked goods
Red No. 40	1971	baked goods, dessert powders, candy, cereal
Yellow No. 5	1969	pet foods, baked goods, beverages, dessert powders
Yellow No. 6	1986	candies, sausage, cereal

Sources: http://www.fda.gov/ForIndustry/ColorAdditives/ColorAdditiveInventories/ucm115641.htm#ftnote3, and http://articles.mercola.com/sites/articles/archive/2011/02/24/are-you-or-your-family-eating-toxic-food-dyes.aspx.

TEXT-DEPENDENT QUESTIONS

1. What are three ways ancient people used additives to preserve food?
2. What is fermentation?
3. What is the function of antimicrobial additives?

RESEARCH PROJECT

Additives are important because food spoils when it comes into contact with oxygen from the air, heat, and moisture. Try this experiment to understand how it works.

What you need:

- 3 pieces of lettuce
- 3 pieces of white bread
- 3 slices of an apple

What to do:

- Place 1 piece of lettuce, 1 slice of bread, and 1 slice of an apple in a sunny spot for 3 days.
- Soak 1 piece of lettuce, 1 slice of bread. and 1 apple slice with water. Let them sit for 3 days.
- Place 1 piece of lettuce, 1 slice of bread, and 1 slice of an apple in a dark spot for 3 days.

Take detailed notes describing what happens. What effect did heat have on each of the 3 bits of food placed in the sunny spot? What effect did moisture have on each piece of wet food? What effect did oxygen (air) have on each piece of food? Was there a difference in the rate of decay for the bread, which is laden with artificial preservatives, then for the apples and lettuce? What can you conclude?

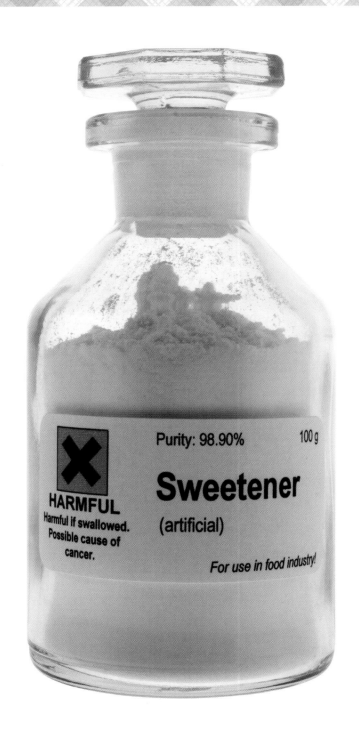

MEDICAL CONCERNS

Words to Understand

antibiotics: medications used in the treatment and prevention of
bacterial infections.

benign: not harmful.

calories: units of energy.

diabetes: a disease that impairs the body's ability to process glucose
into energy.

Trying to figure out what's safe or healthy to eat is not always easy. Many
artificial food additives once thought to be safe were later proven to be
dangerous. Sometimes individual food additives that were benign on their
own were found to create health risks when combined with other substances. The
truth is, it can take years for scientists to find out if an artificial ingredient is safe.
And even then, the results might not be clear.

One of the most intense controversies in recent years involves the use of
antibiotics in the meat and poultry industries. About 80 percent of all antibiotics
sold in the United States are used primarily in processing meat, including beef,
chicken, and pork.

That fact was underscored in a 2012 study published in *Public Health Reports*.
According to the journal, 16 percent of all milk-producing dairy cows in the United

States received antibiotic treatments for a condition called *mastitis*, an inflammation of the cow's mammary gland and udder tissue, while 15 percent of beef calves were injected as a treatment for respiratory infections. Moreover, 88 percent of swine in the United States received antibiotics to prevent a variety of diseases.

Experts warn that the overuse of antibiotics leads to the creation of so-called "superbugs"—germs that have grown resistant to the medications. If a person or animal were to come in contact with such a superbug, it could do a good deal of harm. The overuse of antibiotics in food processing also means that humans are ingesting more of these medications. Over time, humans can become resistant to

A rotary milking system at a modern dairy farm. The use of antibiotics with dairy cows is increasingly controversial.

antibiotics. Consequently, a simple illness—one that was once easily treatable with antibiotics—can turn into a major health issue.

Although the meat and poultry industries says the use of antibiotics "contributes little, if anything, to the burden of human antibiotic resistance," others, such as Consumers Union, a consumer-advocacy group, have concluded that "humans are at risk both due to potential presence of superbugs in meat and poultry, and to the general migration of superbugs into the environment."

THE HEALTH IMPACT OF ARTIFICIAL SWEETENERS

Scientists have also been studying the health effects of artificial sweeteners, including saccharine and aspartame. Food makers use these substances as a substitute for sugar, which can contribute to innumerable health problems, including diabetes, obesity, and heart disease. Accordingly, the global artificial sweetener market is very lucrative, generating around $1.5 billion a year. Food makers use artificial sweeteners in baked goods, powdered drink mixes, puddings, jams, jellies, and other processed foods.

Although artificial sweeteners do not have any calories, they have been linked to several health issues. For example, a 2008 study concluded that those who use sugar substitutes gained more weight than those who did not. The reason was simple: people ate more food loaded with artificial sweeteners, believing the products were better for them.

A 2012 study published in the *American Journal of Clinical Nutrition* concluded that those using artificial sweeteners had more problems with their metabolism (the process by which the body turns sugar into energy) than those who did not use them. Moreover, a 2013 study showed a causal link between artificially sweetened beverages and type 2 diabetes. A 2014 study published in the journal *Nature* found that saccharine changed the function of bacteria in the digestive system forcing the body's glucose levels to rise, and thus putting people at risk for diabetes.

The artificial sweetener called sorbitol. Scientists are still trying to understand the overall impact of artificial sweeteners on human health.

Other studies have found artificial sweeteners to be harmless and safe to consume in limited qualities. The health problems found in other studies may have to do with the amount of the sweeteners being consumed.

THE HEALTH IMPACT OF MSG

Many people over the years have railed against monosodium glutamate (MSG), an artificial flavor enhancer often added to Chinese food, soups, processed meats, and canned vegetables. Although the Food and Drug Administration classifies MSG as a food additive that is "generally recognized as safe," many people claim MSG causes headaches, numbness, heart palpitations, and chest pain.

PUTTING THE 'G' IN MSG

Monosodium glutamate (MSG) is one of several compounds labeled as "glutamates," a group of amino acids that the body uses in the syntheses of proteins. Glutamates are found naturally in many foods, including cheese, milk, meat, fish, and several different vegetables, including tomatoes. It is the substance that gives many of these foods their flavor. MSG is a salt of glutamic acid.

Tomatoes are one vegetable with naturally occurring glutamate; broccoli and mushrooms are two others.

For decades, scientists have been studying whether MSG is bad for human health. During that time, scientists have found no credible evidence linking the flavor booster to any of the maladies associated with its consumption. In 1995 the FDA concluded that while some people might experience some health problems about an hour after consuming MSG, most people did not report any problems.

Another study five years later, involving people who said they had a bad reaction to MSG in the past, cast doubt on their assertions. The study looked at 130 people who said they were sensitive to MSG. Researchers gave them doses of MSG without food, or they gave subjects a placebo, or fake pill. Researchers found only two people had a consistent bad reaction to MSG, and their reactions were also different when they ate food containing MSG. Scientists concluded that those who say they are sensitive to MSG might not be.

THE HEALTH IMPACT OF NITRATES AND NITRITES

EDUCATIONAL VIDEO

FOOD CHEMICALS

Scan this code for a video about chemicals found in almost everything you eat.

Have you ever gone into a grocery store and wondered why meats such as bacon, salami, sausages, and hotdogs look so fresh, even though they spend weeks on the store shelf? These and other processed meats are loaded with nitrites and nitrates, two food preservatives that also enhance color and flavor.

For decades, scientists, doctors, dietitians, and food activists, among others, considered nitrates and nitrites among the worst food additives. Although the preservatives tint meat so it looks fresh and tasty, each has

The additives in hot dogs have been linked to cancer.

been linked to a variety of illnesses including stomach cancer and heart disease. In fact, an environmental watchdog organization called the Environmental Working Group put both nitrites and nitrates on its "Dirty Dozen" list of dangerous food additives in 2014.

However, two 2015 studies concluded that if a person eats a diet rich in both nitrates and nitrites, they might have a healthier cardiovascular system. Researchers found the substances thin blood, widen blood vessels, and lessen the risks for blood clots and stroke. Interestingly, the increased use of nitrates also lowered blood pressure.

BANNED ADDITIVES

 Over the years, a number of food additives have been banned when they were found to pose health risks. A few are listed here.

Additive	Function	Year banned	Health problem
cinnamyl anthranilate	artificial flavoring	1982	liver cancer
coumarin	flavoring	1970	liver poison
cyclamate	artificial sweetener	1969	cancer causing
dulcin (4-ethoxy-phenylurea)	artificial sweetener	1950	liver cancer
ethylene glycol	solvent	1998	kidney damage
monochloroacetic acid	preservative	1941	toxic
nordihydroguaiaretic acid (NDGA)	antioxidant	1968	kidney damage
oil of calamus	flavoring	1968	intestinal cancer
polyoxyethylene-8-stearate (Myrj 45)	emulsifier	1952	bladder stones and tumors
safrole	flavoring (root beer)	1960	liver cancer

Source: Center for Science in the Public Interest, "Chemical Cuisine," https://cspinet.org/eating-healthy/chemical-cuisine#banned.

With such conflicting information, what's a pastrami or hotdog lover to do? First, it's hard to get away from nitrates and nitrites. Even if you don't eat processed meat, both compounds are found in soil, water, plants, and even in our own bodies. When sodium nitrate comes into contact with bacteria, it produces *sodium nitrite*.

While sodium nitrite keeps fat in meat from spoiling and stops deadly bacteria, such as *listeria* and *botulinum*, from forming, when it's heated to more than 266 degrees Fahrenheit, it turns into a compound called *nitrosamines*, a substance that causes cancer in animals. Because of its carcinogenic effects, the U.S. government limits the amount of nitrites food makers can add to meats. In 2010 the World Health Organization listed nitrates and nitrites as possible human carcinogens.

Interestingly, most people do not consume the majority of nitrates and nitrites from hotdogs, salami, or other preserved meat. Instead, about 80 percent of a person's daily nitrate consumption comes from vegetables, including celery, spinach, lettuce, and cabbage. These and other foods pick up the compounds from the soil, which is often laced with nitrogen-based fertilizers.

When a person bites down on a stalk of celery, or chews a leaf of lettuce, the bacteria in that person's mouth converts the nitrates into nitrites. Yet that's not such a bad thing. The body's cells store nitrites until they combine with oxygen. The result, *nitric oxide*, relaxes blood vessels and increases blood flow.

So should a person consume nitrates and nitrites or not? There is some back and forth on the issue, but experts agree that processed meats are not healthful, no matter what preservatives food companies add to them.

RED SCARE

Anytime you walk down a grocery store aisle or stop into a convenience store, your eyes automatically fixate on the vivid colors of food. Snack cakes, taco chips, soda, and candy along with a bread basket of other treats, all seem tastier, and perhaps healthier, because of their vibrant and rich colors. As you read in chapter two, food dyes were originally derived from coal tar, but they are now based on petroleum. Companies use them because they are cheaper and brighter than natural colorings.

Candies depend on artificial colors to get their attractive appearance, but in the past, some unsafe dyes have been used.

In January 1976 the FDA banned an artificial food dye called Red No. 2 because scientists said the substance, known as *amaranth*, might cause cancer. The decision sent off shockwaves around the world, because at the time Red No. 2 was the most widely used artificial food coloring. It was an important ingredient in candy, sausages, and cosmetics.

Although the dye had not been linked to any deaths, its removal set off a near panic. People were so worried about the dye's ill-health effects that consumers forced the Mars candy company to eliminate red M&Ms, even though the candies didn't contain the substance.

Food makers had used the dye for decades, and as *Time* magazine reported at the time, "Without it, instant chocolate pudding would be greenish, artificially flavored grape soda would look blue, and cake mixes would have a lemony-green tinge. . . . About 1 million pounds of the coal-tar-based stuff—a $5 million industry in itself— have ended up annually in more than $10 billion worth of foods, drugs and cosmetics."

In 2008, the Center for Science in the Public Interest (CSPI) called on the FDA to ban all nine artificial food dyes in the United States because of a variety of health concerns, including links to cancer, hyperactivity, and allergic reactions. The scientists at CSPI reviewed the published studies on the dyes and concluded that "these synthetic chemicals do absolutely nothing to improve the nutritional quality or safety of foods."

In addition, CSPI said that some dyes have caused cancers in animals, contain cancer-causing contaminates, or "or have been inadequately tested for cancer or other problems." Specifically, scientists said Blue No. 1, Red No. 40, Yellow No. 5, and Yellow No. 6 caused allergic reactions in some people, while tests on lab animals had determined that Blue No. 1, Blue No. 2, Green No. 3, Red No. 40, Yellow No. 5, and Yellow No. 6 showed signs of causing cancer. Some studies have also linked artificial food dyes to behavioral problems in children.

Each country is responsible for regulating artificial colors. What might be illegal in one country is perfectly acceptable in another. For example, the European Food

Authority said in 2010 that Red No. 2 was safe, although it recommended limiting children's consumption of Red. No. 40, which is used widely in the United States and Canada.

BANNED COLORINGS

 Over the years, numerous artificial food dyes have been banned due to their negative health effects. The chart below outlines some of them.

Artificial coloring	Year banned	Health problem
Butter yellow	1919	liver cancer
Green No. 1	1965	liver cancer
Orange No. 1	1956	organ damage
Orange No. 2	1960	organ damage
Red No. 1	1961	liver cancer
Red No. 2	1976	possible carcinogen
Red No. 4	1976	high levels damaged the adrenal cortex of dogs
Red No. 32	1956	organ damage
Sudan No. 1	1919	carcinogen
Violet No. 1	1973	carcinogen (it was used to stamp USDA mark on beef carcasses)
Yellow No. 1 & No. 2	1959	intestinal lesions (high dosages)
Yellow No. 3	1959	heart damage (high dosages)
Yellow No. 4	1959	heart damage (high dosages)

Source: Center for Science in the Public Interest, "Chemical Cuisine," https://cspinet.org/eating-healthy/chemical-cuisine#banned.

Moreover, some products in Great Britain, such as Fanta orange soda, are colored with natural extracts, including those from carrots and pumpkin, while in the United States the drink's maker uses Red No. 40 and Yellow No. 6. In Britain, McDonald's strawberry sundaes are colored naturally with strawberries, while Red No. 40 is used in the United States.

TEXT-DEPENDENT QUESTIONS

1. What is a "superbug," and where does it come from?
2. What is the main job of glutamates?
3. What were some of the health problems associated color additives that have been banned by the United States over the years?

RESEARCH PROJECT

Research each of these common food additives. List the benefits and drawbacks of each, and then provide your class with an oral report based on your findings.

- aspartame
- BHT
- tartaric acid
- saccharin
- sulfates
- nitrates
- sodium chloride

CHAPTER
4

CONSUMING ADDITIVES

WORDS TO UNDERSTAND

marketing: the way companies advertise their products to consumers.

stipulate: to specify conditions in an agreement or law.

If you take a peek inside your refrigerator, freezer, or cupboards, chances are you will find boxes, cans, and containers of processed food, such as breakfast cereals, instant soups, boxed puddings, frozen pizzas, and soft drinks. Each of these swims in a sea of food additives. You're not alone, of course. In fact, processed foods make up 70 percent of the average American diet.

Why do we consume so much food with additives? The reasons are as varied as the ingredients in each container. For one thing, processed food is less expensive to produce. It is abundant and easy to transport. Processed food also has a long shelf life, which enables people to shop less frequently. For many of us, processed ready-to-eat meals are the answer to a busy world in which there is little time for cooking.

There is an economic component to this also. Grocery stores in low-income neighborhoods are more likely to carry processed foods than stores in high-income areas. That's because people on limited incomes often have to eat whatever is the cheapest.

ADVERTISING

Food makers use slick and colorful advertisements, much of it targeted toward children, to get us to buy their products. In fact, the Federal Trade Commission says the food industry spends up to $10 billion a year marketing processed food to kids. The Rudd Center for Food Policy and Obesity at the University of Connecticut says that cereal, which is high in sugar and fortified with a variety of artificial ingredients, is just one type of processed food heavily promoted to children. In fact, experts at the university say the average child in the United States watches an estimated 13 food commercials on television every day, while teens see more than 16. Most of the products advertised are for high-sugar and artificially enhanced foods, including candy and sugary drinks. In comparison, the Rudd Center says, children see about one healthy food add per week on TV.

The average kid sees about 13 food commercials every day.

WHO'S WATCHING?

As noted above, it is the government's job to protect consumers from dangerous food additives. In 1958, Congress passed the Food Additives Amendment to the Federal Food, Drug, and Cosmetic Act. The amendment stipulated that any substance intentionally added to food is subject to FDA approval unless the substance is generally regarded as safe.

EDUCATIONAL VIDEO

THE FDA

Scan this code for a video about the U.S. Food and Drug Administration.

At the time the law was passed, there were only 800 additives in food. But as the food supply became more diverse, food makers started using more and more substances, increasing the workload of federal regulators. Today, around 10,000 additives are allowed in our food. In 2011, President Barack Obama signed into law the FDA Food Safety Modernization Act to minimize hazards in food.

Despite all these safeguards, most people really don't know what they're eating. Critics of the FDA say the explosion of food additives, coupled with an easing of government oversight in recent years, has allowed food makers ample opportunity to put new, untested additives into their products. In fact, the FDA's deputy commissioner for food admitted to the *Washington Post* in 2014 that "we simply do not have the information to vouch for the safety of many of these chemicals." The commissioner, Michael Taylor, also said, "we aren't saying we have a public health crisis, but we do have questions whether we can do what people expect of us."

How are food makers getting around all the regulations and the oversight process? It seems it's been going on for years. In 1997 the FDA responded to budget cuts by reducing staff. Consequently, there were fewer people to review new additives that came on the market. To get around this enormous problem, the FDA proposed rule changes to make the review process easier. The agency began to allowing

FOOD FAKES

What you eat isn't necessarily what you think you're eating, and if you were to believe a 2016 headline in the *New York Post*, then "everything we love to eat is a scam." Specifically, many food manufacturers are not only putting additives in your food, but they are also substituting one type of food for another without people noticing. The trend has been called "fake food."

For example, in 2016 the TV news show *Inside Edition* reported that the lobster bisque at the Red Lobster chain of restaurants wasn't made from lobster, but contained langostino. Langostino comes from squat lobster, which isn't really a lobster at all; it is an animal related to hermit crabs.

Chefs, whether on television, in restaurants, or at home, love to use extra virgin olive oil in their dishes, especially on salads. Yet many brands of olive oil are diluted with soybean or sunflower oil, not to mention a great many chemicals.

Sometimes red snapper isn't red snapper at all, but tilefish, which is on the FDA's "do not eat list" because of its high mercury content. Mercury is a poison. Lots of times "wild salmon" isn't wild salmon, but salmon raised on fish farms. Honey bought in a store can be cut with other sweeteners such as corn syrup. And grated Parmesan cheese sold in the United States is often a combination of cheaper types of cheese and wood pulp.

According to Larry Olmsted, the author of *Real Food, Fake Food*, fake food is a big problem, especially in the United States. The fraud costs consumers nearly $50 billion a year. One fake honey scam in the United States netted scammers $80 million.

Langostino is a type of seafood that can be very tasty; the problem comes when restaurants pass off langostino as lobster without telling customers.

Critics of the FDA object to the fact that some additives are not tested for safety before being allowed into the food supply.

manufactures to add additives that the FDA "generally recognized as safe" to their products without review. All the companies had to do was provide the FDA with a summary statement of the company's own scientific findings. It cut the approval process from years to months.

According to the Natural Resources Defense Council, most companies used the loophole as a "side door" to skirt the oversight process.

In 2014, a consumer advocacy group, the Center for Food Safety (CFS), took the FDA to court, claiming the agency is failing to protect the public from dangerous food additives. The CFS alleged that more than "250 food additives have entered the food supply based on manufacturer safety claims, without FDA approval, some likely harmful to human health." The CFS claimed that "our nation's food safety agency has become little more than a rubber stamp for the food industry." In 2016 the case was still making its way through the court system.

REFORM AND EDUCATION

While the food industry argues that safety concerns regarding food additives are overblown, many groups have called for the FDA to reform its approval process and get back to the job of protecting the food supply. But at the end of the day, the old saying, "caveat emptor," applies: buyer beware. Ultimately, it is consumers' responsibility to educate themselves.

Activists say people should choose fresh foods over processed foods whenever possible. They should also read labels and question ingredients that they might not have heard of before. People should also know the difference between natural and synthetic additives.

Tatiana Heggestad might have found her own solution. In 2016 the sophomore at George Stevens Academy was asked by a reporter for the *Bangor Daily News* in Maine if she would take a bite of the world's oldest Twinkie—the one that has lasted for four decades under a glass case. "I don't think I would," she said, "it's 40 years old."

TEXT-DEPENDENT QUESTIONS

1. What's the name of the law that gives the FDA power to regulate food additives?
2. What percentage of processed foods make up the typical American diet?
3. What are "fake foods?"

RESEARCH PROJECT

Create a portfolio or scrapbook of magazine and Internet advertisements that illustrate how food makers target their products to young audiences, specifically children and teens. What can you conclude? Share your results with the rest of the class.

FURTHER READING

BOOKS AND ARTICLES

Eschliman, Dwight, and Steve Ettlinger. *Ingredients: A Visual Exploration of 75 Additives and 25 Food Products.* New York: Regan, 2015.

Ettlinger, Steve. *Twinkie, Deconstructed.* New York: Hudson Street Press, 2007.

Farlow, Christine. *Food Additives: A Shoppers Guide to What's Safe & What's Not.* Escondido, CA: KISS for Health Publishing, 2013.

Hennessey, Rachel. "Living in Color: The Potential Dangers of Artificial Dyes." *Forbes.* August 27, 2012. http://www.forbes.com/sites/rachelhennessey/2012/08/27/living-in-color-the-potential-dangers-of-artificial-dyes/#4213fabb3213.

Medline Plus. "Food Additives." https://medlineplus.gov/ency/article/002435.htm.

Schatzker, Mark. *The Dorito Effect: The Surprising New Truth About Food and Flavor.* New York: Simon and Schuster, 2015.

Sifferlin, Alexandra. "Your Fridge Might Be Full of Fake Food." *Time.* July 19, 2016. http://time.com/4412535/food-fraud-olive-oil/.

U.S. Food and Drug Administration. "Cool Tips for Kids: Use the Nutrition Facts Label to Make Smart Food Choices." http://www.fda.gov/downloads/Food/IngredientsPackagingLabeling/LabelingNutrition/UCM410490.pdf.

Winter, Ruth. *A Consumer's Dictionary of Food Additives.* New York: Three Rivers Press, 2009.

WEBSITES

Center for Science in the Public Interest: Chemical Cuisine
https://cspinet.org/eating-healthy/chemical-cuisine
A thorough exploration of safety issues related to a wide variety of additives.

Healthy Choices from Washington's Farmers

http://www.healthychoices.org/just-for-kids_28.html.

A website from the state of Washington's farmers that includes educational activities on nutrition.

KidsHealth.org

http://kidshealth.org/en/kids/nutrition

This site has sections that teaches children about food and nutrition, ways to stay fit, and cooking healthy recipes.

U.S. Food and Drug Administration

http://www.fda.gov/Food/IngredientsPackagingLabeling/FoodAdditivesIngredients/ucm094211.htm

Extensive overview of food additives, including preservatives, sweeteners, colorings, and more.

EDUCATIONAL VIDEOS

Chapter One: WebMD. "Food Additives 101." https://www.youtube.com/watch?v=jSgILz-ZX8I.

Chapter Two: HowStuffWorks. "Canned Food: Where Did It Come From?" https://www.youtube.com/watch?v=5jSXPK73pps.

Chapter Three: SciShow. "5 Chemicals That Are in (Almost) Everything You Eat." https://www.youtube.com/watch?v=3qdnnhgu4FE.

Chapter Four: RegulatoryPharmaNet. "Introduction to the U.S. Food and Drug Administration (FDA)." https://www.youtube.com/watch?v=IjFXAOQyE0w.

SERIES GLOSSARY

amino acid: an organic molecule that is the building block of proteins.

antibody: a protein in the blood that fights off substances the body thinks are dangerous.

antioxidant: a substance that fights against free radicals, molecules in the body that can damage other cells.

biofortification: the process of improving the nutritional value of crops through breeding or genetic modification.

calories: units of energy.

caramelization: the process by which the natural sugars in foods brown when heated, creating a nutty flavor.

carbohydrates: starches, sugars, and fibers found in food; a main source of energy for the body.

carcinogen: something that causes cancer.

carnivorous: meat-eating.

cholesterol: a soft, waxy substance present in all parts of the body, including the skin, muscles, liver, and intestines.

collagen: a fibrous protein that makes up much of the body's connective tissues.

deficiency: a lack of something, such as a nutrient in one's diet.

derivative: a product that is made from another source; for example, malt comes from barley, making it a barley derivative.

diabetes: a disease in which the body's ability to produce the hormone insulin is impaired.

emulsifiers: chemicals that allow mixtures to blend.

enzyme: a protein that starts or accelerates an action or process within the body.

food additive: a product added to a food to improve flavor, appearance, nutritional value, or shelf life.

genetically modified organism (GMO): a plant or animal that has had its genetic material altered to create new characteristics.

growth hormone: a substance either naturally produced by the body or synthetically made that stimulates growth in animals or plants.

herbicide: a substance designed to kill unwanted plants, such as weeds.

ionizing radiation: a form of radiation that is used in agriculture; foods are exposed to X-rays or other sources of radiation to eliminate microorganisms and insects and make foods safer.

legume: a plant belonging to the pea family, with fruits or seeds that grow in pods.

macronutrients: nutrients required in large amounts for the health of living organisms, including proteins, fats, and carbohydrates.

malnutrition: a lack of nutrients in the diet, due to food inaccessibility, not consuming enough vitamins and minerals, and other factors.

marketing: the way companies advertise their products to consumers.

metabolism: the chemical process by which living cells produce energy.

micronutrients: nutrients required in very small amounts for the health of living organisms.

monoculture farming: the agricultural practice of growing a massive amount of a single crop, instead of smaller amounts of diverse crops.

nutritional profile: the nutritional makeup of given foods, including the balance of vitamins, minerals, proteins, fats, and other components.

obesity: a condition in which excess body fat has amassed to the point where it causes ill-health effects.

pasteurization: a process that kills microorganisms, making certain foods and drinks safer to consume.

pesticide: a substance designed to kill insects or other organisms that can cause damage to plants or animals.

processed food: food that has been refined before resale, often with additional fats, sugars, sodium, and other additives.

protein complementation: the dietary practice of combining different plant-based foods to get all of the essential amino acids.

refined: when referring to grains or flours, describing those that have been processed to remove elements of the whole grain.

savory: a spicy or salty quality in food.

subsidy: money given by the government to help industries and businesses stay competitive.

sustainable: a practice that can be successfully maintained over a long period of time.

vegan: a person who does not eat meat, poultry, fish, dairy, or other products sourced from animals.

vegetarian: a person who does not eat meat, poultry, or fish.

whole grain: grains that have been minimally processed and contain all three main parts of the grain—the bran, the germ, and the endosperm.

INDEX

ABOUT THE AUTHOR

John Perritano is an award-winning journalist, writer, and editor from Southbury, CT. He has written numerous articles and books on a variety of subjects including science, sports, history, and culture for such publishers as Mason Crest, National Geographic, Scholastic, and Time/Life. His articles have appeared on Discovery.com, Popular Mechanics.com, and other magazines and websites. He holds a Master's Degree in American History from Western Connecticut State University.

PHOTO CREDITS